Endorsements

"The book had me at 'return your shopping carts.' Holy hells bells, YES. Are you worried that you have a wee bit of dickishness in you? Then grab your copy of *Don't Be a Dick* and make sure you excise all the unwanted things that could make you a dick from your life. Besides being a delightful and funny read, you might actually pick up a few valuable lessons on what it means to be a great person without being a dick."

Dr. Rev. Katy Valentine
ORDAINED MINISTER, NEW TESTAMENT SCHOLAR, AND METAPHYSICAL ENGINEER

"Matthew has written the book that we all never knew we needed! This quick-witted and clever little read is equally mad as it is brilliant, and it is the book I wish someone handed to me and made me read when I was in my 20s, moving out of Evangelicalism and figuring out how to be a human in the world. This admittedly self-help book is a practical guide to humanity in the 21st century West and is a must read for anyone who recognizes the complexities of the times in which we live in, yet wants it told to them like it is—plain, simple, and without all the highfalutin mumbo jumbo. The wit kept me laughing, the wisdom kept me reading. Well done and bravo!"

Maria Francesca French
POST-CHRISTIAN THINKER AND WRITER

"*Don't Be a Dick* is a wonderful mix of brutal honesty and hilarious comedy. I went from cheering on Matthew's points to feeling convicted to do better, and then to rolling over with laughter and back again. Definitely a must read!"

Laci Bean

CERTIFIED TRAUMA RECOVERY COACH

"Complete with golden rules you never knew you needed on just about every topic, from tipping to toilet paper, this book covers it all. Somewhere between comedy and conviction, you'll find the absolutely candid words of wisdom by Matthew J. Distefano in *Don't Be a Dick*. Distefano's cadence and style of delivery make heavy topics such as outdated gender roles, toxic religious culture, and dysfunctional parenting easy to digest. In a time where most of what we see on TV and social media is scripted, embellished, and exaggerated, this book offers a real, refreshing opportunity for self-reflection. If you're committed to being a dick, then this book will offend you, but for the rest of us who know we've got to put in a little more work to become the best version of ourselves, I offer the words of Distefano, 'Trust me, together we can handle this.'"

Desimber Rose

AUTHOR AND SPOKEN-WORD ARTIST

"This is the book that most people will buy for someone else to read without realizing they need it even more themselves. Matt pulls no punches here, and spares no punchlines either. After reading this you'll be a better human being and you'll have fun along the way. Don't be a dick. Buy this book today."

Keith Giles

AUTHOR OF THE *JESUS-UN* SERIES
AND COHOST OF THE HERETIC HAPPY HOUR PODCAST

"When is good to be a dick? When you're an actual penis! Others, just don't be a dick! In his latest book, Matthew J. Distefano takes on the role of a modern-day Emily Post, articulating the kind of etiquette that will save your ass. One of the great problems of the Information Age is that we can say things without fear of getting hit in the mouth. However, we can be banned from social media, fired from our jobs, expelled from school, and otherwise become a pariah in society. Matt, himself, is no shrinking violet—he is a champion for the downtrodden and a voice of reason in theology. He also keenly understands how to be vocal without making a complete ass of himself. In *Don't Be a Dick*, he shows you how to be meek without being weak, how to simultaneously not be a dick while not being a 'limp dick.' If you want to know how to navigate this modern world without being confused with a phallus—while remaining uncompromised in your principles—this book is for you. Matter of fact, this should be required reading in every high school in America!"

Derrick Day

AUTHOR OF *DECONSTRUCTING RELIGION*
AND COHOST OF THE HERETIC HAPPY HOUR PODCAST

Cover design and layout by Rafael Polendo (polendo.net)

Cover elements by lukeruk and RetroClipArt (shutterstock.com)

First Edition

ISBN 978-1-957007-06-9

This volume is printed on acid free paper and meets ANSI Z39.48 standards.

Printed in the United States of America

Published by Quoir
Oak Glen, California
www.quoir.com

69 PRACTICAL WAYS
OF MAKING THE WORLD
A KINDER, MORE LOVING PLACE

MATTHEW J. DISTEFANO

DEDICATED TO MY WIFE LYNDSAY,

WHO PUTS UP WITH MY

OCCASIONAL DICKISHNESS

Table of Contents

SECTION II: HOW TO NOT BE A DICK TO YOUR COWORKERS

SECTION III: HOW TO NOT BE A DICK TO YOUR COMMUNITY

SECTION IV: HOW TO NOT BE A DICK TO PEOPLE ONLINE

Introduction

Why did I write this book? Easy. Look around you. Dicks here. Dicks there. Dicks just about everywhere. But more to the point; too often I am one of them.

That's right, you guessed it! This book is, first and foremost, for myself. It is a reminder that I can be a bit of a dick sometimes. But it's also for you—not for that person you're thinking of right now—you know, the one who cut you off in traffic the other day—but you. Yes you!

And look, you've certainly dealt with dicks in your life. I'm guessing you can probably think of ten people off the top of your head who could use a book like this. But forget them for a moment. Think of all the times you've been a dick.

Of course, I don't want you to now turn around and be a dick to yourself. I don't want the admittance that you can be a dick to be something that brings shame to your life. As my friend Michael often reminds me, grace is always available. So have grace for yourself and just do better next time.

That's what this book is all about. It's not a psychoanalysis into the inner workings of dickery. It's much more practical than that. It's made up of 69 lessons that you can apply today. And yes, I realize that's a pretty crass number, but so what? I'm a man-child. Don't guilt me.

Anyway …

How is this book put together? Simple. It's broken up into four easy-to-read sections: how to not be a dick at home, how to not be a dick at work, how to not be a dick in the community, and how to not be a dick online. Naturally, these lessons will just be covering a handful of practical situations, and should never be a replacement for those of you who need professional help. In other words, if you need therapy for any reason, don't turn to a self-help book like this one. Instead, find a licensed social worker or marriage and family therapist.

That said, please take this book seriously. I know it's pretty cheeky and oftentimes crass. But there are also good nuggets in here that, if applied more universally, would help make the world a kinder, more loving place. Not everything will apply to you, so if you need to breeze by something, I won't be offended. Figure out what works for you. Apply accordingly. And at the end of the day, just be less of a dick than you were yesterday. We're all in this together. No one is perfect. It's all a learning experience. So, learn from your dickishness. I'll learn from mine. And maybe someday soon we'll all see the fruit of our efforts.

Acknowledgments

I would like to thank my lovely wife Lyndsay for everything she does for our daughter and I. She is a one-of-a-kind woman.

Special thanks to my daughter Elyse for making me laugh, smile, and cry, and for making our TikTok so much fun.

A shout out to Michael Machuga—my comrade, best friend, and confidant.

Thank you to the Quoir family and fellow cohosts of the Heretic Happy Hour: Rafael Polendo, Derrick Day, Keith Giles, and Katy Valentine. We've had a blast so far, haven't we?

To Michelle Collins: Thank you for being a great friend and motivation.

My parents, Dave and Sharon, have been really supportive, especially since I came out bi. I owe them a debt of gratitude.

And to everyone else who supports me: Thank you. There are too many of you to mention by name, but you don't go unnoticed. Cheers!

SECTION I:

How to Not Be a Dick to Your Family

1: ON BABY MAKING

Graduate high school, get a degree, then start pumping out babies. That's what my Evangelical Christian culture told me to do. And while I technically followed that order of events, my wife and I waited until we were closer to thirty to have our child.

Not everyone has to wait that long, but most people probably should. And not to be a dick or anything, but some people shouldn't even have children. Look around. Between climate change and the obvious lack of parental skills out there, that much is obvious.

This is one reason why cultural norms don't fit for everyone. Hell, they probably don't fit for most folks. And we've screwed up a lot of people by sticking to them. Couples in their early twenties having kid after kid, only to divorce by their earlier thirties. Gay men and women being told they aren't really gay and then having to confront their spouse and children with the truth later in life. So much unneeded pain and trauma.

To that end, my advice is for you is to wait to have children. Enjoy your twenties. Get rid of debt. Find a career that you enjoy, one that provides a bit of stability. See a therapist for a while, just in case your parents fucked you up more than you'd like to admit. Gain some maturity. Figure out who you are. You might think you know who you are at twenty-two, but you likely don't. Wait. Give it some time. At thirty, you'll still be virile. Probably. And if you don't want to have kids at all, never feel like you have to. Even if you'd make great parents, you don't owe it to anyone.

Reflection

If you have children, when did you have them? Looking back, do you think you should have waited? If you don't have children, are you planning on waiting until you are a bit older? Why or why not?

2: ON BEING HELPFUL AROUND THE HOUSE

You know how men are supposed to work long hours and women are supposed to keep the home? Yeah, fuck that shit. This isn't the 1950s and you aren't your grandparents. Not that we need to shame them or anything, but we've moved on from those norms. They had their cultural context and we have ours, and these so-called gender roles that we are supposed to live under are outdated and unnecessary. If you disagree with me, well, you're probably a dick. And an old dick at that.

Men, I'm pretty much speaking to you here: You've got to help out around the house. And you've got to help with the kids. Newsflash: you don't babysit your kids; they *are* your kids. You raise them. You change their diapers. You feed them when they're hungry. You do bath time when they're caked in mud. You read to them when they're sleepy, and if you're talented like I am, you play for them a Gaslight Anthem tune on the $400 Fender acoustic your wife bought you for your birthday. That's what you do because you're their dad, and you're not a dick. Quit bitching.

Women, don't stand for anything less. You aren't your man's mommy, no matter how much his Freudian ass may secretly want that. At the same time, though, you don't get a pass to do nothing. Ladies, you can be dicks, too, and if you don't want to be one, work as a team and get shit done. Trust me; together you can handle this.

Reflection

Think of a time you didn't help out with what you knew needed doing around the house. How did it make you feel? How did it make your family feel? What could you have done to not be such an unhelpful dick?

3: ON SEXUAL CONSENT

The following sound advice may be triggering for some, but I feel I would be remiss if I didn't talk about marital rape. So, here goes nothing.

First off, it sucks that I even have to mention this, because it's such a shitty thing to talk about. Second, it doubly sucks that I primarily have to talk to Christians about it. Why? Because they are, by and large, the ones who justify this bullshit. You know Paul's phrase, "Wives are to submit to their husbands?"[1] Well, Christian men have been using it to justify having sex with their wives, in spite of the fact that they may not want to have sex at that moment, for far too long. And I'm not talking about Christian men from the 11th century; I'm talking Christian men today—so-called post-Enlightenment men.

Regarding this, then, my philosophy is basically this, and this is something that I live by. And I always have. And I always will. Don't ever, for any reason, do anything to anyone, for any reason, ever, no matter what, no matter where, or who, or who you are with, or where you are going, or where you've been, ever, for any reason, whatsoever, justify rape.[2] I don't care if you're married or not, it is never okay. End. Of. Discussion.

Lastly, ladies (or men, to a lesser degree), if you are in a relationship where things like this occur, seek help. The National Sexual Assault Hotline is 1-(800)-656-HOPE. The National Domestic Violence Hotline is 1-(800)-799-SAFE. They are both available 24/7, and are, of course, completely confidential.

---

1 Ephesians 5:22.

2 If you're wondering about my grammar here, you need to watch *The Office*. That's all I'll say about that.

Reflection

Have you ever been in a situation where marital rape has been justified, either by clergy or otherwise? What counsel was given? How did it impact your life in practical ways? What did you do to gain a healthier perspective on sex?

4: ON SPANKING

Have you ever heard the following? "I got spanked and I turned out just fine?" I have. It's stupid. For one, you probably didn't turn out fine (you're justifying hitting children, after all). And second, sometimes we turn out fine in spite of all the horrible shit that happens to us. I mean, could you imagine the following rationale? "My pregnant mother did meth and I turned out fine," or "My priest touched me when I was five and I turned out fine." Idiotic, right? Same goes for spanking.

So, how are we going to discipline our kids, then? First, by not being a dick. That's the minimum. After that, it's probably gonna take some work. We're going to have to think creatively. We're going to have to reason with our kids. As I've stated many times on social media, if your kids are old enough to understand reason, reason with them, but if they aren't, then they won't understand the reason for their spanking. Either way, don't hit them.

Christians, I know what you're going to say. "Spare the rod and spoil the child." Well, not to be a dick or anything, but if that's how you are going to use the Bible, you'd be better off shoving it so far up your ass that you'll need a colonoscope to find it. You may cause yourself some bodily harm, but at least you'll be sparing your child from the trauma caused by spanking.

Because that's the thing we've figured out about punishment like this; it causes lasting trauma. That's why both the American Academy of Pediatrics[3] and the American Psychological Association[4] are against it. And if you don't want to be a dick toward your children, you'll be against it too.

---

3 https://www.aappublications.org/news/2018/11/05/discipline110518.

4 https://www.apa.org/monitor/2019/05/physical-discipline.

Reflection

Have you ever spanked your children? Did it have the lasting effect you had hoped it would? Do you regret it? Were there better alternatives that you wish you had tried?

5: ON PARENTAL AUTHORITY

Three words that get you nowhere: "Because I said." What does that even mean? I guess it means you are the parent so anything you say goes. But what does that teach your child? Nothing good.

Like spanking, appealing to your parental authority is lazy. It lacks a certain level of creativity needed to properly raise happy and healthy children. "Because I said" is the equivalent of bullying smaller kids on the playground.

And look, we've all probably said this or something similar. Sometimes our kids drive us up a fucking wall and we snap. But this book is about being better at life, so we need to realize when we've succumbed to dickishness.

What, then, do we replace "because I said" with? Natural consequences are a good start. Explain to them why they should or shouldn't do something and what happens when they do the opposite of what is good. Then move into the relational aspect of their decisions. "If you do that, I will feel . . ." Or, "How would you feel if one of your friends was treating you like how you are treating me?" Things like that. Kids are smart. They are intuitive. If you reason with them, they will likely reason with you. If you want them to pick up their toys and they don't want to, explain natural consequences to them: "You won't find your things when you want them." Or, "You aren't gonna like it when your special toys go missing." If they insist on talking back to you, ask them if they like it when people talk back them. Empathy will go a long way here.

Again, "because I said" will only teach them to distrust authority. And sure, on some level, there should be a healthy distrust. But this isn't one of those instances. Get creative and put in more effort than "because I said."

Reflection

Think back to when you were a child and what it felt like to have a person of authority respond to you with "because I said." Would you have been motivated to do what they told you? Did responses like this strengthen your relationship with that person or not?

6: ON SUPPORTING YOUR CHILDREN'S ACTIVITIES

So, you don't like listening to children sing out of key? Or forgetting their lines in a play? Or failing to throw a strike for twenty pitches in a row? I'm with you. But guess what? If you don't attend your children's activities, you are gonna regret it later in life. Trust me. My dad would know.

Here's the thing about your kids: They have their own interests. Their interests aren't always your interests. We all know the stories about fathers who force their sons to play football because back in '78, they starred for their junior varsity high school team. But what if your son is into ballet and not football? Easy. Learn the difference between an arabesque and a plié, between first and fifth positions, and why it's called a pirouette and not a spin move.

Is it obvious my daughter is a dancer? Good. That's the point. I was a baseball player in high school and a hockey player after, but when my daughter took an interest in ballet, I took an interest in ballet. I never wanted to see the Nutcracker multiple times over, or attend dance competitions all throughout California, but now I do. Why? Because I am interested in what my daughter is interested in. I don't make her play sports because I did. That would be a dick move.

So, at the end of the day, in spite of how busy you are, or how tired work made you that day, make time to attend your children's activities. Those will be the memories you take with you throughout life. And before you know it, they'll be all grown up and starting a family of their own. Don't miss out on what's right in front of you.

Reflection

What's your favorite thing to watch your children do? If you don't have children, what's one time you remember your parents showing up to an activity of yours? How did it make you feel? If your parents weren't around, how did them missing out on your life impact you?

7: ON CONSISTENCY

How many people do you know actually practice what they preach? How many people hold themselves to the same standard they hold their spouses? I'm guessing not enough.

I see it all the time. Parents who smack their kids while at the same time telling them not to hit their siblings. Husbands who demand that their wives look like Victoria's Secret supermodels while they walk around like olives attached to two toothpicks. I'm not trying to body shame anyone; I'm talking about being consistent.

A good rule of thumb is that you look to yourself as the role model. If you want your children to be respectful and kind, you can't go around acting like a complete asshole. If you think it would be best for your spouse to work out once in a while, get your sloppy ass to the floor and start doing some ab work. Eat a fucking salad. I don't know, but all I'm saying is that you better clean off your own porch before bitching about your neighbor's.

I believe this is something like what Jesus meant when he told us to view our neighbor's sin as a speck of dust, but our own as a plank. What he was trying to say is that we should hold ourselves to the highest standard. If we don't, it's likely we'll turn into self-righteous hypocrites, bitching about what everyone else is doing while never realizing the giant blind spots we have ourselves. And honestly, that's not a good look. You want others to act a certain way? You better get your ass in gear and be the best damn version of yourself first.

Reflection

Are there any areas of your life that you could improve on before expecting it in others? Do you expect more from your children or spouse than from yourself? How could you go about being mindful of your inconsistencies?

8: ON TOILET PAPER

First off, let me start by saying this: The toilet paper goes over the top of the roll, not underneath. If you put it on the opposite way, then you may not be a dick, but you certainly are a psycho. My wife is a psycho.

To be a total dick when it comes to toilet paper, though, you'd have to not only fail to replace the current roll, but leave the vanity empty as well. That's the ultimate dick move.

Look, it's not difficult to take the extra step to replace the roll. I know it's a pain in the ass to undo the bar, toss the tube, and put a fresh new roll on, but you've gotta do it. There's nothing worse than taking a shit and having nothing to clean yourself with. If your spouse is home, you have to yell for them to drop a new roll by the door, but if you are alone, you have to do that little pants-down-at-your-ankles waddle all the way to the storage cabinet where you keep the extra rolls. It's not a good look, but it's better than vengefully using your wife's tank top out of spite.

Lastly, if you have the money, treat your asshole right and get a nice package of toilet paper. Better yet, do as the Europeans do and get a bidet. I hear that's the way to go. Plus, it's probably better for the environment. Win-win. Your asshole wins. The earth wins. And you have one less thing to accidentally forget to do around the house.

Reflection

Have you ever been stranded on the toilet with no TP? How did you feel? Did you feel like yelling? What did you do to calm yourself down? Have you ever been the one who forgot to replace it, and then had no one to get mad at but yourself?

9: ON TOILET SEATS

For this lesson, I'm mainly talking to those who have a penis. Not because those who don't aren't capable of making an absolute mess in the bathroom, but because those who do typically are the greatest offenders of such grossness.

First off, no one expects others to have perfect aim. Children don't have a lot of practice using their "equipment," so we should all have a little grace for them. The elderly population tends to have "flow" issues, so again, have some grace. However, for everyone, no matter one's age, everything you need to clean up after yourself is available to you (unless someone was a dick and forgot to replace the toilet paper roll). Here's a handy play by play of how things should go:

Stand over the toilet

Pull your dick out

Do your best to aim for the middle

If you miss, or if some splashes, take note

Put your dick away and zip up (carefully)

Wipe down the toilet seat (and the floor if you really got out of control)

Flush

Wash your hands, you filthy animal

That's it. If you can't do that, you're acting like a dick. But since you're reading this, I'm guessing you don't want to be. So, take heed and don't be one.

Reflection

What's the worst toilet scene you've shown up to? How disappointed were you? What did you do to relieve yourself? Did you clean it up, or find a different toilet?

10: ON PUTTING SHIT BACK ON THE SHELF

It's 9 o'clock PM. You need a late-night snack, so you head into the pantry and grab a handful of chips. You empty the bag, but instead of crumpling it up and throwing it away, you put it back on the shelf. Newsflash: That's a dick move.

I hate to admit it, but I've done this. Not often, but it's been done. And I'm not proud of it. Neither should you be.

Now, it's obvious that this isn't the worst thing you could be doing in life. You aren't necessarily harming anyone or being malicious; it's just one of those annoying things that, over time, will likely grind your family's gears. Generally, people don't like clutter. They also don't like picking up after you. So don't make them. Pretty simple, right?

Last thing: If you have your Alexa device (or something similar) keeping track of your shopping list, and you eat the last of something you know you'll need more of, add it to the device. You don't want your daughter yelling at you for eating the last of her jerky without replacing it. I would know!

Reflection

Have you ever been craving something, only to find an empty package on the pantry shelf? Have you ever done this to your family? How did you feel? Did you get a lot of grief over this behavior?

11: ON MANSCAPING

This isn't the 1970s so many of us manscape. If you don't know what that is, then not only is this lesson not for you, but you probably have a bush like a 40-year-old Serbian. Not that there is anything wrong with that; it's just not everyone's favorite look these days (though I hear bushes are making a comeback).

But anyway, fellow manscapers, I'm talking to you here: You *have* to clean up after yourself. You can't just leave your trimmed pubes all over the bathroom floor. Put a towel down. Trim over the toilet or in the shower. Something. Your spouse doesn't want their just-cleaned bathroom sullied by your man hairs. Seriously, don't be a dick when you groom your dick.

I feel like I could leave it at that, but I want to add that you also shouldn't be a dick to yourself in this area. What I mean is that you should treat yourself to a good razor. Don't cheap out and get the $5 ten pack. Those plastic razors are only gonna leave bumps and then, when you're done with them, take like 800 years to break down. Instead, treat yourself right and get the Manscaped Lawnmower 4.0. You'll thank me later, and so will your partner(s).

Reflection

If you manscape, where do you do it? If you make a mess, does it bother those whom you live with? What does flippantly grooming over the bare floor say about you? Do you really want to be "that guy?"

12: ON NAIL CLIPPINGS

This lesson is pretty much exactly like the last one. Pubes. Nail clippings. Pretty much the same premise here.

Obviously, trimming your finger nails is a must. Try not to pick them. In the age of COVID, definitely don't chew them. Clip them, but do so in a responsible and clean way. I like to do it over a sink, or, if I'm fixing the dry shit on my feet, over a towel that I then shake off outside prior to tossing it in the dirty laundry bin. Whatever you choose, don't just leave your clippings on the floor. That's kinda gross and pretty damn unbecoming.

Like everything, it's also a good idea to put shit back where it goes. If you use the nail clippers, don't leave them out or put them where they don't belong. That's a surefire way to annoy the bejesus out of the next person who needs them. If karma means anything, that next person will be you, so take the tiny bit of extra effort required to put the clippers back where you got them.

Reflection

What do you think of when you see a pile of nail clippings on the floor? Do you find it attractive? Do you think it's kind of trashy? Have you ever been responsible for such gross behavior?

13: ON LAUNDRY

I'm not here to tell anyone how to do their laundry—which detergent is best, when to use hot and cold water, and so on. What I am here to offer is advice on how to not be a dick. Here are a few things to consider.

When you throw your dirty clothes in the hamper, unfold them. If you don't, not only will your rolled up socks not get cleaned, but no one—not even your lovely spouse who absolutely adores you—wants to do too much handling of your stinky foot condoms.

Another thing you should do when you have time is fold your clothes and put them away as soon as you can. If you just leave your clean clothes in a pile, your shirts are gonna get wrinkly as fuck, and you don't want to go around town looking like a scrub who can't put himself together.

And lastly, work as a team to get this shit done. Help each other out. Laundry isn't the woman's job. It's everyone's job. They are your stinky-ass clothes, too, Mr. Man.

Reflection

After you do your laundry, how long do they sit in a pile? Do you actually iron your shirts, or just let them get all wrinkly? When you throw your socks in the hamper, do you unfold them or not? Have you considered how much extra work goes into doing laundry when you cut corners? Do you think this annoys your spouse?

14: ON FIGHTING

Every couple gets into disagreements. Stay with someone long enough, and they will annoy you from time to time. Believe it or not, but this is even true of my wife and I.

Sorry, honey.

This reality doesn't mean that you have to fight like angry politicians. Things don't have to get nasty. In fact, fighting with one another can be a great opportunity to model how to respectfully have a disagreement with someone you love.

Needless to say, our children are pretty much always watching us. They probably pick up on way more than we'd like to admit. So, if we are going after our spouses like veteran UFC fighters, then that is going to cause a lot of problems at home. However, if we disagree with our spouses, but do so with respect, then our kids are going to have a model with which to work with when they inevitably get into disagreements with others.

Cool, huh?

Of course, you want to make sure that the disagreements they witness are age appropriate. For example, don't fight about the lack of quality sex in front of your ten-year-old. That would be a dick move, which is something you are trying to avoid. So, keep it on the up and up and make sure you are quite intentional with this one.

Reflection

If you have children, do you get into disagreements in front of them? If you don't have children, did your parents fight in front of you? How did it make you feel? Could there have been a way for them to fight without being disrespectful? How so?

15: ON HEALTH

Your body is your own. This is true. But your relationships are not entirely. They involve, in deeply intimate ways, those you're in relationship with. Duh, right? Well, this means that you probably owe it to them to take care of yourself.

I've had to wrestle with this sobering fact. You see, I used to be a pretty heavy drinker. Not that I was an alcoholic or anything, but I certainly went over the limit recommended by physicians. Of course, I could have probably gotten away with this for years, decades even, but I didn't want to take that risk. I didn't want to continue being a dick. My family deserved better. They deserve to have me around for as long as possible, and so I decided to stack the deck in our favor.

In 2021, I quit drinking alcohol and replaced it with cold-pressed vegetable juices. Beets. Carrots. Kale. Greens. All the good stuff. I also started riding my bicycle all over town, and got in the best shape of my life. Not solely for my vanity's sake, but for the sake of my family.

I recommend you do something similar. Not that you have to cut things out entirely, but at least consider it. Your context is your own, just like mine is my own. Cutting out alcohol entirely was something that I knew would work for me. Maybe you won't have to be so drastic, but please consider taking control of your health, not only for your sake, but for the sake of those who love you.

Reflection

What is one thing you can change today that will make you a healthier person? How can you go about putting such a change into practice? How do you envision it impacting your life? What stops you from making positive changes?

16: ON SEXUALITY

For those who don't know, I'm bisexual. I've also been happily married to a woman for nearly two decades. When I came out publicly, not everyone in my family—more accurately, my wife's—approved of my sexuality. To be perfectly honest, many of them were total dicks about it.

Here's the thing I would want them to consider (as if they read any of my books, but maybe): My sexuality doesn't change who I am as a husband or father. I'm sorry if you think it does, but it doesn't. It just means I find some men attractive. Simple as that. Get over it.

This is the problem with not affirming the LGBTQ community. You set yourself up to becoming a complete dick when those you claim to love come out as anything other than straight. You have it set in your mind what people's relationships should look like, and then when they don't look like that, you end up being a judgmental asshat. My advice? Don't do that.

Now, I can't make you a more affirming and inclusive person. I can only tell you that if you are not, you run the risk of out-and-out dickery. And because you're reading this book, I'm guessing you don't want this to happen. So don't let it. Pull your head out of your ass and join the Light. It's fabulous over here.

Reflection

If you are non-affirming, what prevents you from truly loving your LGBTQ neighbor? Would you want people to not affirm you and your sexuality if it were in the minority? What makes you think it is okay to denounce someone because of who they love, or are even attracted to?

17: ON FAMILY GATHERINGS

For many, family gatherings can be a bitch of an afternoon, especially in today's political climate. My advice? Keep religion and politics out of the conversation. Then thank me later.

Now, I am not opposed to discussing religion and politics with family per se. But you have to first make sure you have the type of relationship that allows for respectful dialogue. Not all family members share this view.

My stepdad and I, for instance, can go at it pretty vigorously and then shake hands at the end of any heated debate. He is way more conservative than I am, but that doesn't matter. We debate. We bicker. We duke it out. And then we shake hands like men because our relationship means more than our political ideas.

Others, however, can't do this. They take shit way too personally, and then act like total dicks to one another, never to speak again. Unless that is your goal, it's probably best to table such discussions until you can be relatively certain they won't be blowing up in your face.

Reflection

Do you talk politics or religion with your extended family? Why or why not? Have you ever had a discussion go completely south? How, if at all, did it get resolved?

SECTION II:

How to Not Be a Dick to Your Coworkers

1: ON COMPENSATION

So, you own a successful business? Well, good for you. I'm sure you've worked really hard to make it. The question is: Do you treat your employees well? Do you go above and beyond in order to show them how much you appreciate them? Do you pay them a livable wage? Or do you just pay lip service?

Because here's the thing: no matter how hard you've worked, other people have helped get you to where you wanted to go. You hired the right staff. You landed the right manager. Things worked in your favor, and as such, you need to compensate your people appropriately.

I'm not just talking to the billionaires who launch themselves into space inside dick-shaped rockets either. Sure, those are the easiest targets. But I'm talking to the local business owners as well—the ones we don't hear about on the news. Y'all need to make sure you aren't taking advantage of us "little people" too.

Not to sound like I'm ass-kissing, but take Quoir Publishing for instance. The owner, Rafael Polendo, has what could be considered a really successful publishing house. How he got there? He always put his authors first. Ask any Quoir author and they'll tell you the same thing. If anyone is a model for success, it's Rafael. He's living proof that you can put your people first and still kill it in the marketplace.

Reflection

Have you ever worked for someone who didn't value what you brought to the table? How did it make you feel? Did it motivate you to give your best effort? If not, what did you do about it?

2: ON CALLING OUT SICK

We are in the age of COVID, so this lesson is more pertinent than ever. I can't stress this enough: if you work in close proximity to other people and find yourself coming down with something, please call out sick. This isn't the time to be showing up to work, coughing up a lung and blowing through an entire box of tissues before lunch.

I know that for some of you, calling out sick is a huge inconvenience. Bills have to be paid. Kids have to get to school. Life isn't gonna stop for you just because you feel like shit. This is why we need good bosses who look out for their employees.

Bosses, you really do need to have compassion for your workers. They need to have plenty of paid sick time. And if not that, they need to have the ability to work from home, should the job warrant it. We've landed rockets on Mars, for God's sake, so I think we can figure out how a good portion of our work force can get shit done from home.

Reflection

Have you ever had a job that didn't encourage you to call out sick, or even shamed you when you did? What did you do when you felt like shit? If your job does encourage people to call out sick, how does it make you feel when people come into the office coughing and sneezing up a storm? Has COVID changed your views on this?

3: ON BRIDGE BURNING

There is nothing like a good "I quit" story. Oh, to be able to tell your cunt of a boss that he can take this job and shove it up his ass! What a feeling that would be!

Here's the deal, though: It's probably not a great idea. I mean, sure, it would feel amazing in the moment. After years of dealing with some arrogant asshole's bullshit, nothing would feel better than telling them to take a long walk off a short pier. But at the end of the day, that's confronting dickishness with dickishness. And you never know, it may come back to bite you in the ass someday.

That's the thing about being a dick. Karma has a way of getting its way. Maybe you tell your boss how he is nothing but a bag of dildoes, but then you find that perfect job and need a reference. Well, there goes those ten years that you spent working for his shitty-ass company.

The best way to stick it to your boss, then, is simply to take your services to where you are more appreciated, and absolutely kill it. Let that chip on your shoulder benefit you and your family. You'll thank me later.

Reflection

Do you have a good "I quit" story? Did it ever come back to bite you in the ass? In the end, was it worth it to tell your boss off? Why or why not?

4: ON WORK ETHIC

No one expects you to win employee of the year every year. No reasonable employer grades their employees on a curve of 100%. However, that doesn't mean slacking off should be your MO either. A bit of balance goes a long way here.

It probably goes without saying, but work ethic is directly tied to compensation. I started this section off by talking about compensation because it's probably the biggest way people are treated like shit at work. Assuming you get compensated fairly, though, make sure you are earning your wage. If you get nickeled and dimed by your company, fuck it, slack off all you want. (I'm kidding, but only kinda.)

Seriously though, if you do slack off, you are probably only hurting your fellow coworkers. I know it's difficult to work hard if your employer doesn't offer fair wages, but still, try to not pass the buck to others who will have to make up for your shitty effort. No one likes to have to go the extra mile just to make up for your lazy ass.

Again, though, if you are an employer, don't let this become an issue. Pay your staff. Don't cut corners. Studies show that you'll actually make more money if you pay your staff more because productivity will generally go through the roof.

Reflection

What is your work ethic like at work? Do you notice a correlation between how much you enjoy your job and how much you are paid, and how hard you work? Would earning a higher salary motivate you to be more productive on the job?

5: ON LEFTOVERS

Bringing leftovers to the office is as ancient a practice as ritualistic human sacrifice. Okay, not quite, but nearly. Unlike ritualistic human sacrifice, however, bringing in leftovers can be a good thing. You save money on lunch, and you don't let food go to waste. However, there is one major pitfall: some food stinks!

This isn't necessarily about an office situation, but I remember attending a live play in which the people sitting directly in front of me brought leftover salmon and steamed broccoli as their snack. The minute that Tupperware opened, holy shit, everyone knew it. Don't be like these clowns.

If you must bring something stinky, have a contingency plan. Buy some candles for the office. Make sure the windows are open. Something! Don't just stink up the joint and pretend like no one is noticing. They are. And they secretly hate you for it.

Reflection

What is one food that you just can't stand the smell of? Has anyone ever brought it to work? If so, did you secretly despise them?

6: ON TRASH

I know this may come as a bit of a surprise to some, but you can't smash down the trash ad infinitum. At some point, no more trash will be accepted by the bin, and you will have to get off your ass in order to take out the bag.

And I know what you're thinking: "Don't we have a cleaning crew who does this for us?" Technically, perhaps you do. But there is no reason you need to wait for them to get to it if the problem is presenting itself to you right now. I know you are probably an important middle-management type, but even you can get your hands dirty once in a while. Plus, the walk to the dumpster out back will be good for you. You know, fresh air and exercise and all that shit.

Trust me when I tell you that I've spoken with maintenance people about this. They all report the same thing. If you smash down the trash enough, it becomes a bitch to get out. So don't do that. You're an adult who is fully capable of taking out the trash. Understood? Good.

Reflection

If you feel the need to smash the trash down until it can't be smashed any more, ask yourself why. If you feel it is someone else's job, put yourself in their shoes and ask yourself how you would feel if someone left you a pile of their rubbish.

7: ON DISHES

If you don't do your dishes, someone else has to. My daughter knows this, but still leaves her dirty dishes on the counter. She's a preteen, so it's understandable. At work, though, that's a whole different story.

Honestly, this is just one of those things that should be common sense. You dirty a dish; you clean it up and put it back. If your office has a dishwasher, then rinse the dish and put it in. When the dishwasher is full, run the goddamn thing.

Most everyone at work is pretty busy most of the time (except for me right now; I'm writing this at work). Generally speaking, people have shit to do, and the last thing someone needs is to clean up after lazy slobs who can't pull their own weight. Don't be that person. Use the dish; clean the dish. End of story.

Reflection

Do you have someone at your work who is notorious for not cleaning up after themselves? Heaven forbid, are you that person? How do they make you feel when they don't clean up after themselves? Do you clean up after them or do you just let it slide?

8: ON COFFEE ETIQUETTE

Most offices have a coffee maker. Most people drink coffee. So, needless to say, the first pot isn't generally gonna cut it. Another will have to be made.

A basic rule of thumb is if you drink the last of the coffee, you make another pot. If you want to go around and ask your coworkers if they are going to want some more, that is fine. Just don't be the person who drinks the last of the coffee, and then leaves an empty pot. That's kind of a dick move.

Also, if you want to take your coffee-making game to the next level, get the blend right. Too much water and the coffee won't be strong enough. Too many grounds and you'll give Linda in accounting heart palpitations. Find the right blend, and take pride in your ability to make a solid pot.

Reflection

Refilling the coffee pot is one way you can go above and beyond at work. What are some other things that you can do to make work a happier place to be for everyone?

9: ON FUNDRAISERS

We get it; your kid is trying to raise money for whatever activity they are a part of. And as their parent or grandparent, they've asked you to sell some sugary shit to the office. Cool. Whatever.

The problem is not that they are trying to raise money; the problem is the way in which some people go about selling things. They will go around and hit people up for $5, only to offer them a half-melted Snickers bar. Then, because all the fundraisers seem to fall on the same week, two more coworkers will follow in tow. I'm sorry, but $15 for a Snickers and two Kit-Kats is a bit much, don't ya think?

To that end, perhaps there is a way of going about all this that doesn't rub your coworkers the wrong way. Maybe allow people to be a bit more discreet. Maybe allow them to not feel guilted into paying up. I don't know, but perhaps you should just make an office-wide announcement and let people come to you. Maybe put out the candy bars and, if you trust your coworkers, a money box they can pay into. Something like that. Because feeling guilted into buying something you probably don't even want is not a fun thing to experience at the office.

Reflection

Have you ever felt guilted into buying an overpriced candy bar from a coworker who is fundraising for their kid? What did you do? Did you snub them, or did you pay up?

10: ON BATHROOMS

Ah, shared bathrooms! The bane of everyone who has a gastroenterological condition. Every workplace has them. Some are better than others. But none of them are ideal. None of them are home.

Because of this, we all have to do our part in keeping them clean. It's not just the job of the cleaning crew who shows up after hours. It's your job, and it's my job. And anyone who disagrees with me is a dick of the worst kind.

Men, you need to aim. Women, you need to properly dispose of your products. Everyone, you need to flush your shit. Twice if you need to. After you're done washing your hands—please tell me you wash your hands—throw away the paper towels. Don't flush them. If the trash can is full, please refer to Lesson 6 of this section.

Take pride in your workplace. Make it a nicer place because of your presence. Don't be an asshole and leave it a mess. Keep it clean. Keep it classy. And if you can't, go fuck yourselves.

Reflection

How do you deal with bathroom situations that aren't ideal? How do you ensure that they are safe and sanitary situations for your bum? Does your workplace have a policy or is it just every person for themselves?

11: ON POLITICS

Talking politics can be fun. It can also be fucking horrific. That's why it's best to not discuss them at work, especially in mixed company. If you are completely certain that things won't go south, I guess there can be room for some dialogue, but probably not even then. Rule of thumb: work and politics don't mix.

Here's the problem with breaking this rule: too many people assume their stance is normative, and all other stances are wrong. This leads people to start talking shit, as if everyone around them will agree with them. I can't tell you how many times people have shit on Black Lives Matter, or the LGBTQ+ community, or single-payer healthcare in front of me, assuming I'd be nodding alongside them. Then I can't help but think, "What about me makes you believe I'll be in agreement with you?" Honestly, it's not a good look, and is awkward as fuck.

So again, don't mix politics and work, especially in today's climate. Things are so heated right now that the last thing we all need is more infighting. Table the discussions you want to have for a later date and time. Then thank me later.

Reflection

Have you ever been in a situation at work where someone whom you disagree with was going off about some political issue? How did you handle it? Did you start arguing, or did you bite your tongue. Why or why not?

12: ON UNSOLICITED OPINIONS

Last year, one of my clients came into my office and told me I looked silly. She didn't like my Red Sox hat. Trying to keep things light and jovial, I asked her if it's because she is a Yankees fan, and she said, "No, you just look silly. You look like a teenager."

Well, la-dee-fucking-da, lady! Who the fuck asked you for your opinion, Karen? I sure didn't. (I kinda wish I said that, but I just kept it to myself.)

This is the thing: if you have an opinion about how someone dresses, how their hair is cut, what music they like, what they are eating for lunch, or any other thing that is none of your goddamn business, you can keep your opinion to yourself.

I know, shocking, right?

To just go around, telling people what you think of them, is a dick move. Unless you are sincerely being kind and have an appropriate relationship with a coworker, then save it. Sure, you can tell Margaret in finance that her new haircut looks nice, or that Steve in shipping has a cool new car, but outside of things like that, kindly shut the fuck up. Things get pretty weird when you tell people they look silly to you. Like, maybe they aren't silly; maybe you're just a tool. Ever thought of that?

Reflection

Has anyone ever given you their unsolicited opinion of how you look? How did it make you feel? Did it offend you? Piss you off? What do you think it says about them?

13: ON SEXUAL HARASSMENT

This goes without saying, but sexual harassment has no business being a part of work life, or any part of life for that matter. But I'm not just talking about Matt Lauering the situation; I'm talking about the subtler forms of sexual harassment, too.

I'll give you an example.

Somewhat recently, I was helping a client through a sexual harassment course he had to take for work. Because of COVID, this was offered online, in the comfort of his home. Because he isn't all that tech savvy, I made sure he understood how to take the course. Now, this client doesn't know I'm bisexual, mainly because I know where he stands on the issue. Throughout the entire course, he was saying horrible things about the LGBTQ+ community, while at the same time complaining that he shouldn't have to take this course because he's not the one who needs it (ironic, don't ya think?). This made for an awkward afternoon, one that would have caused me trauma had I not had the ability to shrug his bigotry off. Unfortunately, it's not so easy for a lot of people.

Of course, this person's dickery is just one example of a more subtle form of sexual harassment that sadly goes on every day in our work places. Don't perpetuate it. Don't stand for it. Check your blind spots. And quit being a dick. Thanks.

Reflection

Have you ever been sexually harassed? What did you do about it, if anything? What fears did you have as you went through this? Have you been able to process it later with a therapist or other professional? If not, do you think you would benefit from professional help?

14: ON MICROMANAGING

I don't know about you, but I hate being micromanaged. It's like, if your boss needs to do any and everything themselves, why are the rest of us even here?

Years ago, I had a boss who micromanaged the entire office. Because of this, nothing got done. Bills were late. Work piled up. Everything was fucking chaos. Not a good situation to be in.

If you are a boss, don't be like this. If you have to do everything on your own, then fine, start a business where you are the only worker. But if you need to hire people to help with getting the job done, let some of that control go. If you want your business to succeed, you'll have to.

We are all adults here, and don't need the work version of a helicopter parent. Not only is it annoying as shit, but it prevents people from actually getting their work done. No one does their best work with a coffee-breathing boss standing over their shoulder. Can I get an amen?

Reflection

Have you ever had a boss micromanage you? Did it help you get your work done, or did things spiral out of control? What was the tone of the office?

15: ON LOYALTY

Given the title of this lesson, you might think that I'm gonna advise people to be loyal to their jobs. I'm not. If an employer doesn't treat you right, get the fuck outta there and find an employer who will. My advice in this lesson is to employers.

Listen, if you own a company and have people working for you for three, five, ten, or even twenty years, then show them that you appreciate their loyalty. Don't take them for granted and think that if they left, you could just replace them with a noob. You can't. You can't replace the expertise. It takes time to build trust and knowledge, so act accordingly.

Some of this harkens all the way back to this section's first lesson. You need to compensate your employees appropriately. If someone works for you for four years, they shouldn't be making the same as those who just got hired on. That is a surefire way to ensure a lot of company turnover. It's also a good way for the quality of work to suffer. So, pay them. Appreciate them. And make sure you do everything in your power to keep them around.

Reflection

Have you ever felt like your company doesn't respect you? How did you respond? Did you quit, or try to push through until things were made right? If you had to do things over, would you change how your responded to such a situation?

SECTION III:

How to Not Be a Dick to Your Community

1: ON TIPPING

Waitstaff don't make much money. Like, at all! So, they rely on tips. Generally, between fifteen and twenty-percent is recommended.

Of course, if someone does an absolutely horrible job, or disrespects you and your family—any form of racism, bigotry, or homophobia—a tip is not necessarily required. But instances like these are so and far between that it doesn't really enter into the equation. Nearly all the time, waitstaff deserve a tip.

Christians, hear me when I tell you this: giving someone a Bible tract isn't a tip. Please don't do this. You are a dick if you do. Replacing someone's hard-earned money with Evangelical propaganda is literally the opposite of being a good, Christian man or woman. Stop it.

To the rest of you, keep doing what you're doing. Appreciate those who serve you. Tip your waitstaff. Tip your barista. Tip your bartender. Tip your massage therapist. If those who serve you go above and beyond, tip generously. And if you can't afford a tip at all, you probably shouldn't be getting services where tips are expected. Just sayin'.

Reflection

Have you ever been stiffed when it comes to a tip? How did it make you feel? Do you think tips should be entirely earned, or should there be a minimum tip that goes up as the service goes above and beyond?

2: ON LITTERING

There aren't many things I hate more than littering. All over America's streets, nearly everywhere I look, there are tons of litter. Literally. Tons. Maybe I'm just super sensitive to it, but it really bothers me.

The worst case of littering I ever came across was when I was volunteering my time, picking up trash alongside a highway, and some dumb fucker—probably driving a vehicle with a "Let's Go Brandon!" flag on it—threw a 7-UP bottle at me. I'm not even making that up. He—I'm guessing a "he"—was such a shitty person that he thought he would give me one more thing to clean up. Motherfucker.

Look, you may not care about the eyesore that is litter, but at least care about your future and your children's future. We are on the precipice of complete climate disaster. Not only is the atmosphere heating up, but our oceans are hurting. Big time. We need to be better. We need to stop using so much plastics. We need to clean up after ourselves. We need to do everything we can to give our future generations a life worth living.

Reflection

Does litter bother you? If so, what are you doing about it? If not, why do you think that is? Think about ways in which you can make this planet a cleaner, more beautiful place.

3: ON SHOPPING CARTS

I've only done this one time, but it annoyed me so much that I had to say something. One day, I was sitting on a curb in a grocery store parking lot, waiting to pick a client up from work. A shopper, after loading his groceries into his truck, pushed the cart over to where I was sitting and propped it up on the curb. Then he walked his lazy ass back to his truck and got in.

I shouted over, "Hey, did you want me to put this away for you? Is that why you sat it next to me?" The shopper laughed.

I continued. "Don't worry, I got you." I then proceeded to walk the cart roughly fifteen feet over to the receptacle. After putting the cart back for the thoughtful patron, I snarkily went on. "I can see why you didn't want to do that. It was a long walk, from the curb all the way to where the carts go. Wouldn't want to get all sweaty!"

The shopper just smiled and drove off.

I'm not sure my sarcasm did any good that day, but at least I felt better about things. And maybe, just maybe, the guy realized how much of a dick he was being.

The takeaway: return your fucking shopping carts (or trollies, if you're in the UK). It's really not that difficult.

Reflection

Have you ever failed to return your cart after using it? Why did you do this? How much time do you think it would have taken to return it to its proper place? How do you think your laziness makes the store employees feel?

4: ON LONG LINES AT CHECKOUT

Have you ever been in a hurry and the person in front of you at the checkout line just won't shut up? I have. It's quite aggravating.

Now, there of course is a chance I'm just a grumpy introvert, but what we need to keep in mind is that there are a lot of grumpy introverts out there. We just want to scan our items, pay the tab, and get the fuck home. Sorry, extroverts.

My philosophy is essentially this: I don't want to be responsible for anyone getting annoyed at me because I took too long in the checkout line. Does an item have a missing barcode? Fuck it, I probably don't need it. Do I have exact change? Doesn't matter, use the debit card. Let's keep this shit moving along so everyone can get home to their families, their sports, and whatever else they happen to be doing that night.

Chatty Cathy, I know you're probably a nice lady, but let's be real here. Sorry if that is coming across as a dickish thing to say—I'm not trying to be mean—but if there are nine people behind you in line and you're taking out your checkbook and chatting about your new passion for knitted sweaters, I'm not sure I'm the one being a dick here.

Reflection

When you are in line somewhere, do you consider those behind you? Are you someone who chats with the worker, regardless of how busy it is? Or do you adjust based on circumstances? Why or why not?

5: ON TATTOO ETIQUETTE

I have a lot of tattoos. Too many to count, in fact. To me, they help tell my story about where I've been, what I've thought, and what's important to me. Not every tattoo is something I'd get again, but I regret none of them. They are a part of what has led me to where I am today.

But please hear me when I say this; tattoos are not something to be touched, especially when they are fresh. As an introvert, I don't even want to talk about them with strangers, regardless of how "cured" they are. But I especially don't want you grabbing them and asking me about their meaning.

No joke, but this happened to me once. My forearm tattoo was maybe two days old. Some stranger on the street legit grabbed it, turned my arm so she could see the whole thing, and asked me what it was. I retorted, "A fresh new tattoo so let go of my arm." She didn't like that, but I didn't care.

If you've never had a tattoo, you may not know this (but you still should). Tattoos hurt. You are essentially giving yourself an open wound that takes a few weeks to heal. So, for someone on the street to grab them? Well, that's just stupid. Don't be that person.

Reflection

Do you like it when strangers ask you about your tattoos? Do you find it uncomfortable? Do you think your answer is based on whether you are an introvert or an extrovert?

6: ON MERGING

I'm not sure how many people know this, but where I live—California—the right of way belongs to the person already on the highway. Meaning, the person merging into traffic should adjust their speed in order to slide in.

Of course, that doesn't mean you should be a dick and not let them in. If you can speed up or slow down in order to let someone in, great. If you can move over to let multiple mergers in, perfect. But at the end of the day, the one merging needs to put in some effort, too.

Too often, it seems that most people have it backwards. They pay no mind to anyone around them and drive onto the freeway at twenty miles an hour under the speed limit. Only after they get in the lane do they speed up. Consider me not impressed.

This is the thing about any kind of driving: you aren't the only one out there. Stop acting like you are. Notice the other cars. See what they are doing. See how you are affecting them. Make adjustments accordingly. If you can't handle this, maybe get an Uber. Text a friend. Take the bus. Something.

Reflection

Do you consider everyone else when you drive, or do you just zone out and go through the motions? Would you consider yourself to be an active driver or more of a passive one? Has it always been this way or have things changed over the years?

7: ON BLACK PEOPLE'S HAIR

I'm not Black, but I feel like I know enough to give some advice when it comes to their hair. Stop asking to touch it!

White lady, I know you probably have fine intentions. I know you're probably just curious. But seriously, just stop it.

First off, your hands are probably dirty. One study I read indicated that only two-thirds of Americans wash their hands after using the bathroom. Nasty. COVID or not, that's just fucking gross.

Second, you probably don't want *your* hair touched, so why are you gonna put a Black person in a position where they have to have theirs touched? This behavior only reinforces the stigma that non-Black is normative, and Black is some sort of aberration.

Lastly, and piggybacking on point two, when you ask to touch a Black person's hair, you put them in a position where they either have to let you, or run the risk of being seen as the "angry Black person." This has an historical context that goes back centuries, and this too needs to be destigmatized.

If you don't believe me about any of this, just go read an article written by a Black person. Not sure where to find one? Just Google, "Should I ask to touch a Black person's hair?" I'm sure you'll find plenty of reasons not to.

Reflection

If you are Black, have you had anyone ask to touch your hair? How did it make you feel? If you are not Black, have you ever thought about what it would feel like to be on display for people who were curious about you?

8: ON SMILING

Ladies, have you ever heard this? "You'd be prettier if you smiled more?" My wife has. It sucks.

If it were me, I'd probably say something just as dickish right back. "Well, you'd be a cooler person if you weren't such an asshole." But I'm trying to do some self-work, so I do my best to not say things like that as often as I used to.

But for real, saying things like this to women is uncalled for. None of them are asking for your unsolicited opinion, so save it. Maybe they don't want to smile right now. Maybe something serious is on their mind. Maybe it doesn't matter what you think is pretty or not. Maybe the world doesn't revolve around you. Ever think about that? Obviously not.

So, as you go about your day, don't worry about who is smiling and who is not. You're not the smile police, so don't pretend to be. If you want to see more smiling, do kind things for people. Some are bound to smile at you if you pay for their coffee, or donate to their food shelter, or even if you tell a funny joke. But no one is going to smile, unless sarcastically, if you tell them they will be prettier for having done so. They'd be more likely to tell you where you can stick that smile.

Reflection

Ladies, has anyone ever told you that you need to smile more? How did it make you feel? Men, have you ever told a woman this? What was your motivation? What was your justification for offering your unsolicited opinion?

9: ON MOVIE THEATERS

It's Friday night. You show up to the movie theater, absolutely geeked that the film you've been dying to see is finally out. If you're Keith Giles, it's probably *Dune*. If you're like me, it's *Star Wars*. Either way, you're there and you're psyched.

Then it happens. That *one family* sits right behind you. Immediately, their nasty-ass shoes are mere inches from your head. A thirteen-year-old boy, between chomps of popcorn, is talking loudly about God knows what. His parents don't seem to give a shit. Either they don't hear him or they don't care that he's being a little punk. Now, you have a choice: either put up with their bullshit or say something.

Ask yourself this: are you *that* family? Are you the family that can't shut up during the movie? Are you the type to put your feet up even though someone is directly in front of you? Yes? Then stop it! No? Then carry on, you beautiful person, you! Enjoy your movie. Enjoy your popcorn. And thanks for making everyone's night out more tolerable.

Reflection

What's the worst experience you've ever had at a theater? What happened? How did you handle it? Were you a dick in response to someone's dickery, or did you maintain your cool?

10: ON GYM EQUIPMENT

Unless you're at the gym for the sole reason of looking good on your Instagram page, you are gonna sweat. If you're like me, you're gonna sweat a lot. So, that means you need to be conscientious about the equipment you're using.

I realize that all gyms have house rules, but not all gyms have enough staff to enforce them. Sometimes the gym is dead, and there is no one around but the girl at the front desk. They have cameras, sure, but probably no one to monitor them. That's where self-awareness comes into play.

To be clear: it is okay to sweat on gym equipment. What's not okay is failing to wipe it down. No one wants to touch your funk. Worse yet, no one wants ringworm (yeah, look that shit up if you don't believe me).

I'm not talking about some quick wipe, either. Get the spray bottle. Spray the seat and the backrest. Give it a solid wipe before moving on to the next machine. Anything less is stepping into the realm of dickishness.

Reflection

If you work out at the gym, do you make sure to clean the equipment after every use? If not, have you ever considered that you may be passing on infections to others? Is this something you really want to be unaware of?

11. ON THE HUMBLEBRAG

If you're gonna brag, just brag. If you think you've got that sticky-icky, then just come out and say it. It's much more sincere than trying to play coy about how humble you are.

Essentially, a humblebrag is a boast that is disguised as a humble statement or subtle complaint. Some examples might be:

"Damn! I didn't expect to sell so many books. How the hell am I gonna keep up?"

"What is going on? I'm wearing sweats, didn't even do my hair, and y'all still gonna hit on me?"

And then there's my favorite:

"It wasn't me killing it up there; it was the Lord working through me."

The thing is, when you humblebrag, most people see right through it. You may think you're showing humility, but really, it's just an insincere form of showing off. So, again, if you're going to show off, then own it. Tell the world how many books you're selling, thank the fans, and let it be what it is. Tell Twitter how good your ass looks in sweatpants. If you're a worship leader, write good music and own that shit. Got it? Good. Glad we had this chat.

Reflection

Have you been guilty of humblebragging? Did you think you would get away with it? Did anyone call you on it? What do you think it is about owning something that scares people from just saying it like it is?

12: ON ESCALATORS, DOORWAYS, AND AISLES

I grouped these three items into one lesson because the same shit happens with all of them: people stop in the middle and act as if no one else on the planet exists but them. And my God, is it fucking annoying!

I don't know if it's just me, but I try to avoid getting in the way of others as best I can. If I am on an escalator and don't want to walk, I move to the side in case someone does. If I need to stop and check my phone, or if I forgot my keys, I move out of the doorway. If I'm in a shopping aisle and need to look at the shelves, I pull to the side. I don't just stop my ass short and take up the entire goddamn aisle. That would be a dick move.

But too many people don't seem to give two shits about getting in others' way. They'll just stop in the middle of foot traffic, causing everyone to pile up behind them. Why would they do this? I wish I knew.

Here's a pro tip: treat aisles and doorways like roadways. You wouldn't stop your car in the middle of the road for no good reason, so don't do it in the grocery aisle. Sorry, but if you don't heed my advice and I hit you in the Achilles tendon with my shopping cart, that's on you. Maybe you'll learn from your scuffed-up heel.

Reflection

Are you a "stop wherever I am" type of person? Or, do you take a moment to "pull over" in aisles? Do you talk in doorways or leave them open for the rest of us? Do you even think about these things?

13: ON GROCERY SHELVES

We've probably all done this. I know I have, and I'm not really proud of it. You'll be shopping and you see something you think you want. So, you'll put it in the cart. But then, a little while later, you see something that is similar, but looks even better. What do you do? You put the new item in the cart and put the old item on the shelf wherever you happen to be standing.

I know this is tempting, but it's a bit dickish. It would be nearly as easy just to walk your lazy ass to wherever you got the original item, but instead, you just drop it off where you're at and wash your hands like Pontius Pilate after Jesus' sentencing.

Here's the thing: someone has to clean up after you. And sure, they work there so they get paid for it. But you're an adult, for God's sake, and no one should have to clean up after you like that.

Return your items. Don't make anyone do extra work because you're lazy or entitled. Be a team player. And don't be a dick.

Reflection

Have you ever returned items to places they don't belong? Do you feel a sense of guilt as you attempt to slyly walk away from the "crime scene?" How did it make you feel?

14: ON PASSING GAS

Everyone farts. I've heard estimates that we do it between five and fifteen times a day. I know people who do it far more often. If I get contaminated by gluten, I would be one of them. So, it's a normal bodily function.

That said, there needs to be a protocol to passing gas. I've known too many people who will bust ass wherever and whenever they feel like it. In my car. In a line at the pharmacy. In an elevator. And I'm not just talking about little kids who haven't perfected the art of the private fart, I'm talking about grown-ass adults who don't seem to give a fuck.

I've had social-work clients who have done this. We'll be driving down the highway to some place they need to go, and all of a sudden, my car will fill up with the ungodliest of smells. Or, I'll be helping one of them with a book-writing project, and just like that, their room will begin to smell like the sulfur at Bumpass Hell in Lassen National Forest. I mean, I appreciate how comfortable they are around me, but I don't want things to be *that* comfortable.

So, take it from me; no one wants to smell your nasty ass. Excuse yourself if you need to fart. Go outside. Use the bathroom. Just don't do it in front of others so flippantly. It's awkward, and it's foul.

Reflection

Do you excuse yourself when you need to pass gas? What do you think of others who don't? Do you think it's no big deal, given that we all fart? Or, should there be some ground rules?

15: ON ELEVATORS

In our previous lesson, we talked about passing gas. So, I'll start by saying this: don't fart on an elevator. Just don't. It'll linger for far longer than you think.

Outside of that, there are other ways in which you can avoid being a dick on an elevator. The first is to follow the rule, "off first, then on." Meaning, let those who are already on the elevator exit, then get in. Too many times in my life, I've seen people try to do it the opposite way. They'll try to jam into the elevator before anyone has the chance to get off. How the hell does that make any sense?

Another good rule of thumb to follow is if the elevator is already pretty packed, just wait for the next one. There is nothing worse than having to have your crotch jammed up against some stranger, or to have to smell some mouth-breather's foul breath. It's much more pleasant to have some space between yourself and the next guy, so just wait for the next lift.

Lastly, just always be courteous. Hold the door. Help someone with their luggage. Ask which floor they need. If you do things like that, you just might make someone's day.

Reflection

Have you had any horrible experiences on an elevator? What was it? How could it have gone better? Were you the culprit, or did someone else create the issue? How did you handle it?

16: ON ORDERING

Have you ever been to one of those restaurants where you stand in line to order? Of course you have. We all have. Is there anything worse than someone who doesn't even try to figure out what they want prior to getting up to the register? Not many things.

Look, you don't have to be completely prepared to order prior to getting to the front, but at least put in some effort beforehand. Sure, you may have a few questions. There may be some clarifications needed from the sixteen-year-old student behind the register. But at least have an idea of what you want going into it.

I've seen it way too many times. Someone will be ahead of me and they'll spend the whole time in line on their phone. They won't even look up until they get to the front. Then they want to ask all these questions that are pretty self-explanatory. They'll be at Chipotle, like, "Do y'all have burritos? Yes? Well, what kind of meat can I get?"

It's on the fucking board!!! Jesus!

Sorry, this just annoys me. Don't be that guy. Thanks.

Reflection

When you order, do you try to figure out what you want prior to getting to the front? If not, do you think this helps things move along or not? How could you be more prepared to expedite the process for everyone?

17: ON BIKE PATHS

I ride my bicycle all over town. Generally, I try to get in between fifteen and twenty miles, four times per week. When the bike paths are empty, I have a great time. When they are full, however, it's kinda hit or miss.

Here's what the problem tends to be: people take up the whole bike path as if no one else is around. It's sort of like how people walk down the grocery store aisles. They don't move over when people come up behind them. They don't walk in a straight line. It's crazy.

To that end, if you are an outside walker or bicyclist—and I recommend both, really—pay attention to your surroundings. Treat the bike path sort of like a roadway. If you are going to make a left turn, for instance, look over your left shoulder first. Don't just start walking to your left and then act completely shocked that someone else may be out and about. It's a surefire way to get yourself and others really, really hurt.

Lastly, if you are a speed demon, let it rip when no one is around. If there is a lot of traffic, slow the fuck down. This isn't the Tour de France and you're not in a time trial.

Reflection

Do you enjoy bicycle and walking paths? If so, are there any concerns you have? What have you noticed out there? Are people generally safe or could they be better about sharing the roadways?

18: ON TEXTING

Texting while driving is a horrible practice. That much is clear. But what about texting and walking? Or texting while people are trying to talk to you? How about texting while ordering food or coffee?

A good rule of thumb is this: texting can wait. Listen, I'm as guilty as anyone of being on my phone too much. But please be careful and courteous when on it. I've heard stories of people walking out into traffic while staring down at their screen. I'm sure people have blown out their knees after accidentally stepping off a curb. And when you're in line or someone is trying to talk to you, it's just plain rude.

Again, texting can wait. If it's an emergency, you probably aren't texting the person anyway. You'd be calling them. Put the phone down for now, and come back to it at a later time. Trust me, the internet will still be there, and the person awaiting your text isn't gonna get pissed off if they have to wait an extra 30 seconds.

Reflection

Do you text and drive? Text and walk? Text and order? If so, what is your motivation for doing so? What would it take to get you to change your habits?

19: ON LOUD VEHICLES

We get it, you love your loud-ass car. You spent thousands on that stupid exhaust system—the one with the muffler that sticks out the side. And you want the entire world to know you have arrived. I'm sure you're not insecure at all.

Here's the thing, though—and I'm sure this is gonna be damn-near impossible for you to understand—not everyone cares about your loud car. In fact, most of us find you completely annoying, even out-and-out objectionable.

Honestly, what's the point in revving your engine after every red light? Does it give you that tingle in your dick that you've longingly missed for years? I just don't get it.

Further, have you not figured out by now that the climate is kind of fucked? I mean, I know it's not spiraling out of control because of your yellow Chevy Camaro, but the way you drive certainly isn't helping things.

At the end of the day, who the hell am I to tell people what kind of cars to drive. All I'm asking, though, is for you to respect others. Some of us can't stand loud, abrupt noises. Folks with autism have it especially bad. So, calm the fuck down, Trevor. That girl you're trying to impress isn't gonna fuck you because of the size of your muffler. It's the size of your . . . compassionate heart . . . women care about.

Reflection

What are your thoughts on loud cars? If you are a proponent, do you stop and think about how others might view them? Do you care? Or is it not your problem?

20: ON DOGS

I get it; people love dogs. I mean, I don't get it, but I get it. I have two of them, not because I want to, but because my wife and daughter outnumber me. And while they can be fun, they are often quite annoying (the dogs, not my family).

Now, I realize that I'm probably in the minority here, but that's okay. I'm not asking anyone to get rid of their dogs. If they are great companions for you, then have as many as you want (within reason). My only request is that you don't assume everyone wants to be friends with your canine companion.

One thing that bugs me more than most things is a dog that jumps on me. I know, like everyone says, the dog is friendly. I don't care. I don't like their slobber and I don't like their dirty paws. Plus, the only time I was bitten by a mangy mut was by one who was supposedly "friendly."

Also, if your dog is a barker, that is understandable. Just please try to do something about it. Take them to classes. Put them inside. I really don't care what you do; just don't let them bark and bark and bark every time I am outside in my yard. That's obnoxious.

And lastly, for the love of everything holy and sacred, pick up after your pooch. And I don't mean putting the shit in the baggie and then leaving the baggie on the sidewalk. I mean carrying the shit-filled baggie with you and throwing it away when you get back home from your walk. Capisce?

Reflection

Are you a dog lover? If so, what do you do in order to make sure that those of us who aren't feel comfortable around you and your pets?

SECTION IV:

How to Not Be a Dick to People Online

1: ON VIRTUE SIGNALING

The working definition of virtue signaling is "the public expression of opinions or sentiments intended to demonstrate one's good character or social conscience or the moral correctness of one's position on a particular issue." My definition is telling the world how great you are but not actually doing shit to make it a better place.

Often, white liberals get accused of doing this. And let's face it, they are totally guilty—throwing up a #BLM on their Twitter profile pic, posting a pro LGBTQ+ article during Pride Month, etc. Conservatives are just as guilty though. They just have different moral codes that they adhere to, often corresponding to whatever church denomination they belong to.

Of course, there is nothing wrong with talking about the things you're doing to make the world a better place. The problem is that for many, it's all talk and no game. So, my advice is this: if you're gonna talk shit, you better live it out. If you are gonna talk about how black lives matter, start supporting black-owned businesses. Speak out against the war on drugs. Vote to end it. Choose candidates who are for prison reform. Don't just put on a good show; live your convictions in real time.

Reflection

If you talk a big game, do you actually back it up with boots on the ground? If not, what is holding you back and how can you go about changing that?

2: ON NOT COMMENTING

Did you know that if you come across an online post that you don't agree with, you don't have to comment? I know it's hard to believe, but it's true.

Because I say something like this a lot, I often get accused of desiring an online echo chamber, where every follower of mine thinks exactly alike. This couldn't be further from the truth. I say this, not to dissuade commenting, but to dissuade the type of commenting that leads to a fruitless discussion.

Here's what I mean.

I could post something about vaccinations, or biblical interpretation, or philosophy, and someone I never talk to will say something like, "I disagree." Okay, well isn't that grand? Now, if they wanted to expand on their thoughts, that would be one thing, but they often don't. They just want the world to know that they disagree with what one moron like myself said on Facebook.

Well, isn't that special.

A good rule of thumb is this: if you aren't gonna enter into a serious dialogue with someone, it's best to just keep scrolling, just keep scrolling.

Reflection

If you're like me, you've probably broken this rule. What is it about telling someone that you disagree with them that makes us feel so good, so honorable? Do you find yourself struggling to just scroll past stuff you don't agree with? Why do you think this is?

3: ON TOSSING GRENADES

I'm gonna admit something with you: I do this all the time—I'll think of something that I know will rile people up, and will post it on my page right before signing off for the night. The next morning, I'll wake up to 74 notifications, 3 personal messages, and a pitchfork-wielding mob outside my bedroom window (okay, not quite).

This is sort of a dick move, and accomplishes nothing constructive. The problem for me is that I get a kick out of it. But such is often the case when we are being dicks.

A better, less dickish approach is to make sure you're available to monitor the fallout after a contentious post. This requires planning, but is well worth it.

The worst offense one could make is tossing grenades on other people's posts, or in groups that you are in. This is a big no-no. Only toss fuel onto a fire if you are gonna stick around to deal with the blazing inferno. Otherwise, save it and live to start shit another day.

Reflection

Have you ever had someone toss a social media grenade onto your post, only to ghost you immediately after? How did it make you feel? Did it cause frustration? What do you do about things like that?

4: ON DOXING

Doxing is a tricky subject. For the most part, doxing someone—revealing private information about them in order to publicly shame or extort—is a total dick move. Not only can it ruin lives, it can ruin the wrong lives if your information is shit. My personal stance is that I don't engage.

However, there are probably instances where doxing can be a good tool to keep people in check. Take, for instance, the recent Texas abortion ban. In this bass-ackwards excuse for legislation, random citizens can sue for up to $10,000 if they think anyone aided a woman in getting an abortion. That's some fucked-up shit right there. So, would doxing them be an appropriate response? Some would argue it is.

I hesitate to affirm such a practice because violence will inevitably ensue. Not always, but certainly at some point. It may start with public shaming, but as these things are wont to do, it may escalate. So, again, that's why I don't personally engage, and why I suggest you refrain as well.

Reflection

Have you ever doxed someone? Have you ever been doxed? In each scenario, how did you feel? Are you sure you released the correct information? If your personal information was shared, was all of it correct? What was the fallout?

5: ON REPLYING TO ALL

I work at a company where pretty much everyone uses the "reply to all" feature when responding to group emails. This annoys the bejesus out of me. I'll come to work after being off for the weekend, and I'll have twenty-something emails, and nineteen of them have nothing to do with me or my department. Ugh!

But more than that. Because of the clutter this "reply to all" practice creates, when I *do* get an email that pertains to me, it sometimes gets lost in the weeds. Then I have to explain to my supervisor how I didn't see the email because I had a nine-email-thread about Debbie's seven-year work anniversary. Sorry Debbie, but while I appreciate your dedication to your job, I don't really need to read all the congratulatory emails from corporate. I'm sure you can understand.

So, please be mindful about how you respond to group emails. Do your best to just reply to the sender, unless of course everyone needs to read your response. Your coworkers will appreciate it.

Reflection

Does this practice annoy you as much as it does me? Are you guilty of hitting "reply to all" every time you receive a group email? Could you be more mindful in this area?

6: ON TYPING IN ALL CAPS

Have you ever come across a comment on social media that was in ALL CAPS? I have. Too often. There is a common theme in all of them—the commentor is angry, uneducated, ungrammatical, and secondhand embarrassing. Plus, HAVE YOU EVER TRIED TO READ SOMETHING IN ALL CAPS IT'S REALLY DIFFICULT AND YOU AREN'T SURE WHAT THE PERSON IS EVEN TRYING TO SAY BECAUSE THEY TYPICALLY RUN ON AND ON WITHOUT THE USE OF COMMAS OR OTHER FORMS OF PUNCTUATION BECAUSE THEY ARE JUST ANGRY AND THEY ARE GOING TO LET YOU KNOW ALL ABOUT IT.

Don't be this person. Ever. Unless you want to come across as a total dickbag, avoid AT ALL COSTS! I have nothing more to add.

Reflection

Do you type in all caps? Why? Do you think it is helpful and gets your point across? Have you ever come across someone typing in all caps who actually made sense?

7: ON TONE POLICING

Experts say that eighty percent of communication is nonverbal, which means that communicating online is very limited. You can use emojis, which help, but tone is rarely picked up on.

To that end, a good rule of thumb is to not attempt to police someone's supposed tone. Everyone communicates differently. Some are very expressive while others, like myself, are more deadpan. This style of communication can be seen as off-putting, but it's really just misunderstood.

I get this all the time. I'll be engaged in an online dialogue and someone will inevitably tell me to check my tone. Why? Because I communicate very directly at times, and don't always use emojis. But them telling me that my tone is inappropriate is a huge assumption on their part, and is often just plain wrong. Plus, it's technically an informal fallacy (ad hominem) so really has no place in a dialogue.

I know this can be difficult, but let people's tone be what it is. Online communication is difficult enough to begin with, so worrying about how you perceive their tone of voice should be the least of your concern. Stick to the words themselves and try not to deviate.

Reflection

What are your thoughts on how tone comes through over social media? Do you concern yourself with how someone "seems?" Or do you try to stick to the actual words being said? How has your approach benefited or hindered you?

8: ON SCREEN GRABS

If someone says some crazy-ass shit on a completely public forum and you take a screen grab of it and share it, that's totally fine. If, however, someone says something in a private group you are in and you share it outside of that group, that's a dick move.

I've been in situations like this. It happened in our Heresy After Hours group that is directly affiliated with the Heretic Happy Hour podcast. Someone didn't like what was being said in our private group, so they took screen grabs and shared it to their public Facebook page. When this is done, trust gets violated. It's like sharing a private conversation with the world at large. In essence, it's no better than gossip.

I don't know why people feel the need to violate trust like this, but it happens all too often. The best thing to keep in mind is what I said at the top: only share things that are completely public already. At that point, they are fair game. Keep the private shit in the private groups.

Reflection

Are you concerned that things you say in private will be shared with the wider world? Has this ever happened to you? How did it make you feel, and were you able to trust the person who did this again?

9: ON LAUGH REACTIONS

In the past, I've been guilty of clicking the laugh reaction on stupid-ass Facebook posts. I mean, how tempting is it to laugh at someone who thinks the earth is flat, or that dinosaurs are fake? Super tempting. The answer is super tempting. But look, in spite of how funny that actually is, it's kind of a dick move to do this.

We are in a time in which tensions are high. Divisions cut across just about every section of society. Misinformation abounds. So, the last thing we need right now are behaviors that further alienate large portions of the population. Clicking the laugh reaction is one of these.

Instead, ask people questions. Ask them why they believe the earth is flat. Ask them how many people would have to be in on the conspiracy to cover that up. Ask them what their endgame is. Ask them really hard questions that gets them to think. And refrain from mocking them. Mocking them will only force them to dig their heels in further, and while that can be entertaining to watch, I think it's time we start to move on from the misinformation campaigns of obviously delusional people.

Reflection

Have you been guilty of mockingly laughing at people who post stupid shit? Have people done this to you? How did it make you feel in each scenario? Did quality dialogue happen after such a thing was done, or did things spiral after that?

10: ON GISH GALLOPING

The Gish gallop is a rhetorical technique used by people who are attempting to overwhelm their opponent's argument, without regard for the accuracy or strength of their own arguments. The second cousin of the Gish gallop is what I call machinegun questioning, where someone asks question after question after question, resulting in the same overwhelmed opponent.

I'm sure you've come across people who use these techniques. Hell, in the past, I've been guilty of doing it myself. Generally, it's when a fundamentalist Christian makes an asinine claim about the Bible, and I fire off ten to fifteen challenging questions which leads to them being overwhelmed and condemning me to hell. I'm not saying I'm proud of doing this, but sometimes it *is* fun.

The thing is, though, it doesn't actually change anyone's mind. It just frustrates them and makes you look like a bit of a dick. A better approach is to put forth one or two solid arguments or questions, and stick to these until the person you're debating addresses them. If they don't, then move on because you aren't gonna get anywhere.

Reflection

What are your thoughts on the Gish gallop? Have you seen it used in online arguing? Has it led to good discourse or not? Why do you think this is?

11: ON USING SARCASM

Sarcasm is like salt. It's a needed ingredient, but too much and it will offend the palate. Too little and the conversation will be too bland.

When you are in the online space, you need to be careful with how much sarcasm you use. As we've discussed, tone is damn-near impossible to notice. Same goes with sarcasm. If you are gonna use it, then it's probably best to use the wink emoji, or lay it on with people you're close with. Strangers and mixed company probably aren't gonna appreciate your sarcasm as much as you'd like.

Now, you can of course not give a damn if people like it or not, but just beware that that approach may come back to bite you in the ass. You may end up pinning yourself into a corner where everyone viewing the conversation sees you as a total dick. You don't want to go there.

My advice? Find balance. Use sarcasm like comedians use punchlines. Too much and it loses its power. Too little and you're no longer funny. But just enough and you'll be using to your advantage.

Reflection

How do you view sarcasm? Do you use it on a daily basis? Do you find it offensive? Do you even "get it?" How have you managed your own propensity to be sarcastic, as well as those you dialogue with?

12: ON GHOST ACCOUNTS

Ghost accounts are fake accounts people use in order to spy on others after they've been blocked. It's a bullshit tactic done by people who need to get a fucking hobby.

I've come across a few people who have used ghost accounts. One such person was printing out my Facebook posts and showing them to my wife's conservative fundamentalist family. Another was using their ghost accounts to gather fodder for their online blog. Both people doing this were being total dicks.

If you get blocked by someone, just accept it. It's not the end of the world. I've blocked countless trolls and haters. I've likely been blocked by a bunch of religious people. And that's okay. I have no desire to create an account for "Matthew Distefanski" so that I can see what people are saying. I would ask that everyone follows that rule. If you don't, you are being a total creeper, and no one likes a creeper.

Reflection

Have you ever been tempted to create a fake account so you can spy on people? If so, how do you think it would make people feel? If you haven't done this, has it been hard to accept that you've been blocked by those whom you used to communicate with?

13: ON MISINFORMATION

Misinformation is everywhere. Say something with confidence, provide an unvetted source of any kind, and people will latch onto it. Turn it into a meme, and they'll likely share it far and wide. This is the day and age we live in.

I've been guilty of sharing misinformation. Sometimes you come across something juicy and don't have a lot of time to factcheck things. Then you're later forced to admit your error and delete your post. It's embarrassing.

A good rule of thumb is if you don't know if something is true or not, assume it's not and refrain from sharing. If you have time to factcheck and understand how to research like an historian or scientist, then share away. If, however, your research consists of watching some shitty YouTube video your cousin Eric sent you, then please, for the sake of the rest of us, shut the fuck up. As of writing this, people are literally dying because of misinformation being spread about COVID-19, so apologies for being a dick, but you really need to stop. Thanks.

Reflection

Have you ever had to rescind something you've shared because you found out that it was inaccurate? How did you feel about that? What personal checks and balances have you set up to make sure you don't spread misinformation?

14: ON MASS TAGGING

I used to get tagged alongside 100 other random people on Facebook posts I couldn't give two shits about. It drove me up a fucking wall, and unless I actually knew the culprit, I would just unfollow or unfriend. I think people got the hint, which is why it doesn't happen any longer.

As a practice, this is pretty rude. Not because your post isn't valid in some sort of way, but because you didn't get consent to flood others with notifications that they probably don't want. Of course, if you have consent to tag people in things, go for it. Just don't do it too often. As always, balance is key.

But if you're just tagging 100 of your so-called friends in a post about where to save money on authentic Ray-Bans, then you're being rather dickish. And if it's a post about the MLM you just signed up for, there is no "rather" about it. You are simply being a dick. A huge, dirty dick. No one wants to sign up for your MLM. Most are gonna lose money. And no, it isn't a sure thing if you'd only work hard enough. So, please stop asking me to sign up.

Reflection

When someone tags you without your consent, how does it make you feel? Is there a difference between someone tagging you in something they think you'd actually like and if they are just tagging random friends? How so?

15: ON SHARING REQUESTS

I donate to causes as much as I'm able. But I always make sure to vet the agency that receives my money. Personally, I like to give to the Preemptive Love Coalition. But there are countless others who do great work.

So, when someone comes along and asks me to give to their friend's GoFundMe, I get a little put off. What's even worse than a personal request like this is when people try to use my platform to get me to share something of theirs to my fans and followers. This, I really don't like.

And look, I'm trying really hard to not be a dick here; it's just that it's awkward to be put in a situation like this. I use my platform in a very specific way, and while your cause may be fantastic, I would like to make that decision for myself. And I don't want to be seen as an asshole if I decide I don't want to share something.

To that end, instead of asking people to share something, share it on your own page. Join groups where this is allowed, and share there. This is what I do to promote my own work. I have a few pages on Facebook. I join groups and try to engage on there. I share articles I think are related to the milieu of the group. Rarely do I personally ask anyone to share anything.

Reflection

What are your thoughts about people who use the platforms of others to promote something of theirs? Do you agree that it's off-putting? Or, do you see no problem with it. Why or why not?

16: ON FACEBOOK GROUPS

Facebook groups are a wonderful way to engage with like-minded people. But they are not without their faults. Because of this, there are a few good rules to live by.

If you are going to engage in groups, follow their rules. If you don't like their rules, don't be in the group. There are thousands and thousands of groups, so if one isn't right for you, walk your happy ass right out the door.

Second, don't share private things outside of the group. As we talked about earlier, this is like gossiping about private conversations. It's not a good look.

Third, don't add people to groups without their consent. I used to get multiple adds per week, and it drove me nuts.

Fourth, don't cause such waves that the admins have to get involved. Group admins don't make money. They volunteer their time because they believe in whatever the group happens to be about. Again, if you can't play nicely in a group, just leave.

And lastly, when you do leave, don't announce it. No one gives a shit that you're about to leave. Just quietly walk out the door and move on with your life. Shitting all over every member of the group just prior to leaving will only come back to bite you in the ass someday. You know, because karma.

Reflection

Have you had positive experiences in Facebook groups? What are some things you do in order to, not only respect the group, but stay sane in the midst of chaos?

17: ON OLD POSTS

We've all said stupid shit in the past. When I get those Facebook memories from ten years ago, half the time I cringe. Be honest, you do too.

Because we all probably acknowledge this, don't go digging up people's old posts in order to shame them. I know this is a favorite tactic of cancel culture, but it's a total dick move. It's demeaning and allows no room for personal growth and development.

Admit it, if we could dig up everything you've said over the past twenty years, you'd be embarrassed as fuck. And that's okay. This applies to all of us.

So, please keep this in mind. If someone is still a piece of shit, then it'll be clear. They'll have said something stupid in the last 24 hours. You don't need to go back to their Twitter posts from 2009. Who the fuck cares what they thought then? They could be entirely different people by now.

Just try to always assume the best in people. Assume they've grown up. If they haven't, then use discernment and judge where they are at today. If it's not up to your standards, then put up some healthy boundaries. Going back a decade is pointless. Just don't do it.

Reflection

Have you ever had someone bring up what you used to believe in order to shame you? How did that make you feel? Did anything fruitful come from it?

Always remember:

BEING A DICK
WON'T MAKE YOURS
ANY BIGGER.

BE KIND,
DO GOOD,
LOVE WELL.

LIFE IS SHORT,
SO START LIVING IT.

For more information about Matthew J. Distefano,
or to contact him for speaking engagements,
please visit *www.AllSetFree.com*

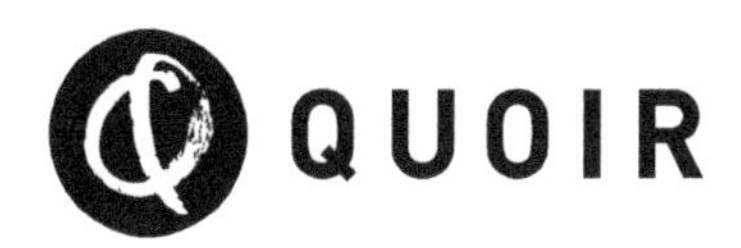

Many voices. One message.

Quoir is a boutique publisher
with a singular message: *Christ is all.*
Venture beyond your boundaries to discover Christ
in ways you never thought possible.

For more information, please visit
www.quoir.com

CPSIA information can be obtained
at www.ICGtesting.com
Printed in the USA
BVHW090951250322
632203BV00004B/1383